We Seek After These Things

Understanding the Young Women Values

AMELIA HAYCOCK

Covenant Communications, Inc.

Cover and interior illustrations © Rebecca Miller

Cover design copyrighted 2007 by Covenant Communications, Inc.

Published by Covenant Communications, Inc.
American Fork, Utah

Copyright © 2007 by Amelia Haycock
All rights reserved. No part of this book may be reproduced in any format or in any medium without the written permission of the publisher, Covenant Communications, Inc., P.O. Box 416, American Fork, UT 84003. This work is not an official publication of The Church of Jesus Christ of Latter-day Saints. The views expressed within this work are the sole responsibility of the author and do not necessarily reflect the position of The Church of Jesus Christ of Latter-day Saints, Covenant Communications, Inc., or any other entity.

Printed in Canada
First Printing: November 2007

14 13 12 11 10 09 08 07   10 9 8 7 6 5 4 3 2 1

ISBN 13: 978-159811-497-3
ISBN 10: 1-59811-497-2

Introduction

The purpose of the Young Women organization of The Church of Jesus Christ of Latter-day Saints is to help each young woman "come unto Christ" (Moro. 10:32; *Church Handbook of Instructions,* 211). The Personal Progress program is designed to assist young women in achieving this objective. Personal Progress is based on seven Christlike values—each with a corresponding color—that young women are challenged to develop and exemplify.

This book is intended to explore the Young Women values through the colors that have been chosen to represent them. These ideas do not represent any official Church stance on the subject, although various Church leaders have published their personal insights on this topic (see "134 Years Young!" *New Era,* Nov. 2003, 24). It is my intention to give the reader one perspective and hopefully inspire her to integrate these values more fully into her everyday life.

As members of the Lord's Church, we are to seek after things that are "virtuous, lovely, or of good report" (A of F 13). The seven Young Women values and their symbolic colors can help us recognize these things. I am truly grateful for the Young Women organization and all it has added to my life, both as a youth and as an adult. I am also grateful for these seven colors that ever remind me to stand for truth and righteousness in all that I am.

Amelia Haycock

Faith

*Faith is the white of
Sacred clothing
So pure and clean—
Blessing, baptism, and temple.*

The first of the Young Women values is Faith. Faith in the Lord Jesus Christ is also the first principle of the gospel (see A of F 4) and is the foundation for all the other values. Faith gives us the desire to live these values to their fullest.

The color representing faith is white—beautiful, pure, and clean. There are three very important times in your life when you will be especially pure and clean. These are times when the Lord desires that you receive sacred blessings and ordinances according to His plan for you. It is your faith that leads you to these points in your life—each time dressed in symbolic, sacred white clothing.

Birth

As a premortal daughter of God, your faith in Jesus Christ led you to come to this earth. You were born a tiny, innocent baby, clean and pure. Even if you were not born into a family who taught you the gospel from your birth, you still came to this earth as a valiant daughter who bravely chose to follow the Savior's plan. Most infants born into Latter-day Saint families are dressed in white and then given a name and a blessing.

It's amazing to hold a precious newborn and look into their eyes, pondering the fact that their spirit has just come from the presence of our Father in Heaven. We are here to build on the foundation of faith we developed before we came.

We have been sent to earth by a Father in Heaven who loves us very much and wants us to learn and grow. Because we no longer live in His immediate presence, our trust in Him grows as we learn to walk by faith and not by sight. He can see our potential for greatness and has given us a plan that, if we have the faith to follow, will allow us to become more like Him.

Baptism

As we grow from year to year, we learn more of our Father's plan for us. And with faith in that plan, we are prepared to dress in symbolic white again as we enter into the covenant of baptism and receive the Holy Ghost. We are then clean and pure once more.

With this covenant of baptism, we promise to take upon us the name of Christ and always remember Him. As our faith continues to grow, we learn to hear the Holy Spirit and allow Him to guide us. Faithfully acting upon these promptings will help us make wise choices, allowing our spirits and bodies to remain clean and pure. In the years that follow, we take the sacrament each week to renew and remember this baptismal covenant, repenting of any unclean thing we have done.

The Temple Endowment

As we move from childhood toward our adolescent years, our faith grows stronger as we learn to rely upon the Savior in joy or pain. Our faith keeps us valiant and repentant, prepared to make and keep further sacred covenants. Then, if we have kept our baptismal covenant, we are prepared to dress in white again and enter the House of the Lord.

Because we are faced with so many temptations, challenges, and obstacles during these years, it is vital that we continually seek to increase our faith. The Lord promises us that we can "withstand every temptation of the devil, with [our] faith on the Lord Jesus Christ" (Alma 37:33).

Faith—pure, clean, and white—is a powerful force. "The Lord is able to do all things according to his will, for the children of men, if they exercise faith in him" (1 Ne. 7:12). Just like when we exercise our bodies, exercising our faith makes it stronger and more powerful. We need strong faith in the Lord Jesus Christ in order to accomplish our "sacred and glorious purpose. [We] have the noble calling to use [our] strength and influence for good" (*Young Women Personal Progress,* 1).

Examples of Faith

There are many powerful examples of faithful women in the scriptures, including the unnamed widow at Zaraphath. She lived at the time of the prophet Elijah when there was a terrible famine in the land. On the day Elijah found her, she was gathering wood for a fire. She told the prophet she was going home to prepare a meal with her last bit of food, so that she and her son might "eat it, and die" (1 Kgs. 17:12). Elijah asked the widow to use the last of her oil and meal to make a cake—first for him, and then for her and her son.

This faithful woman knew she did not have the ingredients to make enough for them both, but she also knew the power of faith in the Lord. What courage she must have had, thinking she would serve her son his last meal and then wait to die of starvation. What a difficult request to consider, giving away her son's final meal. Yet because this widow acted on her faith in a prophet of God, she was then able to "eat many days. And the barrel of meal wasted not," remaining full until the famine ended (1 Kgs. 17:15–16).

In a very real sense, this woman's faith saved her son's life as well as her own. This kind of faith is nourished and fed through prayer, study, service, and acts of kindness, like feeding a hungry prophet of God. Because she did so, the widow also fed herself and her son both physically and spiritually. Faith—pure, clean, and white—*is* a powerful thing.

Each one of us came to earth with this kind of faith. We now have the opportunity to increase that faith through exercising it, as did the widow. Our modern-day "barrel of meal" may be the test of letting go of a negative group of friends, or of holding on with love to a struggling family member. Whatever our challenges may be, we can draw upon the power of our faith in the Lord Jesus Christ, "for in his strength [we] can do all things" (Alma 26:12).

Divine Nature

Divine Nature is the blue of
The clearest sky
Reminding me of my heavenly home.

The second Young Women value is Divine Nature. "We believe in God, the Eternal Father" (A of F 1), and we know we are His daughters, literally. This knowledge helps us remain valiant and true. The color for divine nature is blue, which is what we see as we turn our eyes to the heavens.

"The Family: A Proclamation to the World" states, "ALL HUMAN BEINGS—male and female—are created in the image of God. Each is a beloved spirit son or daughter of heavenly parents, and, as such, each has a divine nature and destiny." We can look into an endless blue sky and feel a sense that there is more to our existence than this tiny world we live on. It is a common saying among us that we are not human beings having a spiritual experience, but spiritual beings having a human experience. Our earth life is temporary. Heaven is the home of our spirits.

Living in the World

There are many women and young women alike who live as if they know who they are and where they've come from. You may know some of these women; hopefully you are one of them. We can recognize these women by the way they live. They know they were not born *for* this world, but merely *into* this world, temporarily. And their values are high because they hold *heavenly* values. Sister

Margaret D. Nadauld, former Young Women general president, spoke of the need for more women like these when she said:

> Women of God can never be like women of the world. The world has enough women who are tough; we need women who are tender. There are enough women who are coarse; we need women who are kind. There are enough women who are rude; we need women who are refined. We have enough women of fame and fortune; we need more women of faith. We have enough greed; we need more goodness. We have enough vanity; we need more virtue. We have enough popularity; we need more purity. (*Ensign,* Nov. 2000, 14)

When we let our divine nature shine through in our daily living, it is apparent to everyone around us—not necessarily that we are different, because we are all children of God—but that we *know it* and *are changed by it.* The world is always around us, ever ready to take up more of our time. School, the media, and even friends and activities pull at us from different directions and compete for our attention. Similarly, the Lord is also always there, inviting us to give Him more of our time and attention. We can do so in many ways. As much as we've heard it before, the Sunday School answers are eternal answers. Personal prayer, scripture study, attending church, and even what we do at home will bring us close to the Lord and enlighten us.

Seeking the Lord First . . . and Always

Because we know that we came from a heavenly home, and we know that we will return someday, young women who understand their divine nature do not invest too much time or attention in this temporary world. Instead, they seek the Lord first . . . and always.

One woman in early Church history had a testimony of her divine nature and helped many others realize theirs. Sister Eliza R. Snow shared her knowledge of God through the way she lived, worked, and used her talents. Sister Snow was a very talented poet. Even today her poems and hymns continue to touch her readers and help them to grow.

She was instrumental in many Church endeavors. Baptized in 1835, she helped to convert her brother, Lorenzo Snow, who became the fifth president of the Church. She taught school in Kirtland and Nauvoo, was the first secretary of the original Relief Society, and later the second general president of the Relief Society. She also helped organize the Mutual Improvement Society and the Primary organization. But perhaps the most important thing Sister Snow has left us with is her testimony. We can gain strength from her feelings about the Savior through the hymns she penned.

The message within her widely loved hymn, "O My Father," provides a reverent glimpse into our divine nature, and illustrates Sister Snow's deep understanding of that nature.

> *For a wise and glorious purpose*
> *Thou hast placed me here on earth*
> *And withheld the recollection*
> *Of my former friends and birth;*
> *Yet ofttimes a secret something*
> *Whispered, "You're a stranger here,"*
> *And I felt that I had wandered*
> *From a more exalted sphere.*
> (*Hymns,* no. 292)

Sister Snow did not have an easy life. Along with many of the early Saints, she witnessed much strife and heartache. She was driven from home to home and lost many loved ones. Sister Snow would have been very close to many of the early prophets and would have felt their pain as they were threatened, persecuted, and even killed. But through it all she never forgot who her true Father really was, and what she was capable of because of that royal genealogy. She knew that this life, no matter how wonderful or sorrowful, was only temporary, and that she was "a stranger here." She reached for the divinity within her and relied upon it for strength.

A Bit of Heaven

When we come to earth, we bring a bit of heaven with us. It is in our nature: we are heavenly. Our Savior created an amazing blue sky which draws our eyes upward, reminding us of that wondrous place from whence we came. As we carry this knowledge with us throughout our lives, it will guide us back to His presence to dwell with Him again. As daughters of God, we echo Sister Snow's words concerning this day.

> *Then, at length, when I've completed*
> *All you sent me forth to do,*
> *With your mutual approbation*
> *Let me come and dwell with you.*
> (*Hymns*, no. 292)

Individual Worth

Individual Worth is the red of
A single rose—
Bold, unique, and beautiful.

The color representing Individual Worth is red, like the deep, bold hue of a precious rose. Each red rose is different, but each has a beauty all its own. Its velvety, curled petals combine with its pleasing scent, bringing happiness to all those blessed to enjoy it. Each young woman is also different, but each is loved and of great worth to our Savior, for He died for *all* mankind (see A of F 3).

As daughters of God we share the same Father, but we're each created individually and have *individual* worth in His eyes. Like each petal of a rose, each young woman has many intricate traits that combine to make her whole person lovely, bringing joy to everyone blessed to know her.

The color red is extraordinary. It can be strong and powerful, making a confident statement about its presence. It can also be gentle and graceful, its crimson hues reminding us of love and devotion. So it is with each righteous young woman. There are times throughout our lives when we need to boldly stand for truth and righteousness. And there are times when we exemplify Christlike love through quiet service and humility. Each of us contributes to the Lord's kingdom in our own unique way.

When each individual rose is combined with others, the collective beauty creates a striking and beautiful bouquet. Although the scent of a single rose is divine, a bouquet adds even more beauty and fragrance to a room. Likewise, when beautiful, confident, and righteous young women gather together for a good cause, their power increases exponentially. Daughters of God with different gifts and talents can combine to make a wondrous bouquet.

In Doctrine and Covenants 18:10, the Lord emphasizes that "the worth of souls is great in the eyes of God." The Atonement of Jesus Christ is evidence of our worth to the Savior and the Father; the next verse reads, "For, behold, the Lord your Redeemer suffered death in the flesh; wherefore he suffered the pain of all men, that all men might come unto him." And verse 13: "And how great is his joy in the soul that repenteth." That God underwent unspeakable and infinite suffering just to give us the opportunity to return to Him loudly proclaims that we are indeed of infinite worth to our Brother and our Father in Heaven.

Consider the story of a woman in the Savior's day who, although imperfect, was so convinced of this truth that she acted boldly, yet humbly, at the same time (see Luke 7:36–50). Hers is a story of someone who, although the world considered her an outcast and unworthy of their respect or even compassion, believed she was of great worth to the Lord.

This woman, who obviously had a strong desire to be forgiven, boldly approached the Lord while He dined at the home of a Pharisee. The Pharisees were considered to be extremely learned and righteous; unfortunately, many were also judgmental and unforgiving. This repentant woman came into the house and sat at the feet of the Savior, crying many tears—maybe of regret and sorrow, maybe of joy to be in the Savior's presence. Her heartfelt tears fell on the Lord's feet. She humbly washed them and dried them with her hair, then went on to anoint the Lord's feet with precious oil.

She must have felt relief and joy that her offering was accepted by Him. She may have been seeking this opportunity for some time. She must have known deep down, that no matter what her sin, her Savior still considered her of great worth. And of course we know Jesus loved her and wanted to help her, even though not all present thought her worthy.

The Pharisee who invited the Lord to eat with him observed what was happening, and he thought to himself that Jesus must not be a true prophet or he would know this woman was a sinner and unworthy to touch Him. Jesus knew what the man was thinking and told the Pharisee that this woman had treated Him with more love and honor than the Pharisee himself had. The Savior then turned to her and said, "Thy sins are forgiven . . . go in peace" (Luke 7:48–50).

Imagine what might have happened next in this woman's life. Although her strong sense of self-worth gave her the confidence to approach the Lord in spite of her imperfections—with her sins now forgiven and her confidence completely restored, imagine the good she was able to go forth and do. She must have stood a little taller that day. She must have shone a little brighter. Perhaps she felt a greater desire to add her unique gifts and talents to the bouquet of so many other righteous daughters of God. Our worth is also great because we are daughters of God, unique and individual, and even greater because we are made perfect through our brother, Jesus Christ. We love and honor Him even as she did.

The Personal Progress booklet emphasizes that we each have a divine mission to fulfill (see *Young Women Personal Progress,* 26). The Lord has custom-designed our personal missions according to our unique talents and strengths. We chose to accept these long ago and promised to do our best to use them humbly, yet boldly. As we stand together as daughters of God engaged in His work, we can know that, collectively and individually, we are of infinite worth.

Knowledge

*Knowledge is the green of
A living tree
Whose growth has made it strong.*

We believe that knowledge is essential to our salvation. In order to return to our Savior we must keep the laws and ordinances of His gospel; obviously to do so we must learn of these laws and ordinances (see A of F 3). As we gain knowledge, we are able to grow both in body and in spirit. Knowledge is the key to achieving our full potential. President Gordon B. Hinckley said, "None of us knows enough. The learning process is an endless process. We must read, we must observe, we must assimilate, and we must ponder that to which we expose our mind. I believe in improvement. I believe in growth" (*Teachings of Gordon B. Hinckley,* 298).

Green is the color associated with knowledge and is reminiscent of a tree's new growth. Trees grow toward heaven if they are free of disease and nourished with light and rain. Each tree begins from a small seed. Although the wind may blow and the storm may rage, if that tree has strong roots and branches, it will stand to see another day. Each of us begins this life with little knowledge, but planted here on earth we can be nourished with intellectual light and reach greater heights. This light, or knowledge, will see us through life's storms and help us enjoy the beautiful todays and tomorrows that Lord has in store for us.

One of the core reasons we come to earth is to gain knowledge and experience that will enrich our lives and spirits. Through studying the holy scriptures and the words of prophets and apostles, through reading good books and enjoying uplifting media, through attending church and seminary with the intent to learn and grow, and through getting "all the education [we] can," we are able to successfully learn what we need to know in order to do what we need to do (Gordon B. Hinckley, *Ensign,* July 1998, 2).

What to Do with It?

And what is it we need to do with our knowledge? We must "stand as witnesses of God at all times, in all things, and in all places," and we must learn of Him in order to do this. We need to move the gospel forward through missionary work and example. We must learn the gospel to do that. We need to become righteous wives and mothers in Zion. This endeavor also requires much learning. There is so much to learn! And when our minds are free from worldly clutter and full of worthy knowledge growth is possible, because the Lord can work through us. Like a green tree reaching for the sun, we will grow spiritually tall as we heed the Lord's counsel to "seek learning, even by study and also by faith" (D&C 88:118).

Young women are constantly learning and growing. The rate and direction of that growth is determined by the choices we make. Many things can introduce disease to our minds and spirits, and there is a lesson we can learn from this. Like a growing tree, sometimes it is necessary to train our branches and guide their growth, pruning back and protecting against some of the negative things that fight to surround us so that we may grow straight and tall. Avoiding corruptive influences and seeking out good and wholesome knowledge will help our spirits to grow tall—and even blossom. This is a part of our Heavenly Father's plan for each of us.

Never a Waste of Time

During our adolescent years when everyday learning is intense and constant, it is sometimes hard to picture the far-off future, much less the eternities. But one day we will carry all the things we have learned with us into that eternity. Too many of us waste too much time and energy in this life pursuing things that are only temporary and which will eventually be of no worth when this life is over. Seeking wisdom and knowledge, however, is never a waste of time.

All the material things of this life—clothes, cars, houses, and toys—will not be worth even the smallest amount of knowledge we have gained when we leave this life and return home to our Father. In fact, many will probably regret the time they have lost in pursuing these worldly, expendable things when they could have been gaining valuable knowledge to last forever. Be bold in your pursuit of knowledge. You will never regret learning good things. You will understand and grow in mind and spirit. This is what the Lord wants for each of us.

Latter-day Saint pioneer Emmeline B. Wells serves as an inspiring example of a woman who continually sought after knowledge, both temporal and spiritual, from her youth. At age fourteen, Emmeline was not only flourishing in the secular realm, graduating from a prestigious private high school in her Massachusetts community—but she was also rapidly gaining spiritual knowledge, and was baptized a member of the Church in that same year.

As she married and had a family, her education continued—raising her five daughters alone as a widowed mother. Although she taught a family school for a time and continued to write poetry, Emmeline's learning for the next twenty years was primarily gleaned from the unparalleled education that only motherhood can provide. Surely she taught her daughters of the importance of gaining knowledge; she is famous for the well-known declaration, "I believe in women, especially thinking women."

Later in her life she served as editor for the Latter-day Saint publication *Women's Exponent,* and used that publication for thirty-seven years to speak in favor of educational opportunities for women, as well as to spread the word about the good works of Relief Society. Known for her keen intellect and executive abilities, in 1876 Sister Wells was appointed by Brigham Young to chair a grain-saving program, which eventually received personal commendation from United States president Woodrow Wilson. She was the first Utah woman to receive an honorary degree and was eulogized as the state's "foremost woman."

Sister Wells quest to seek and apply knowledge, both temporal and spiritual, never ceased. Her commitment to growth allowed her to become a powerful instrument in the Lord's hands, and she made an unforgettable contribution to building the kingdom of God—the results of which linger still today. (See "Emmeline B. Wells: A Fine Soul Who Served," *Ensign,* July 2003, 16.)

Alma the Younger counseled, "learn wisdom in thy youth" (Alma 37:35). Now is a great time to expand your mind! There is much to learn every day, and young women all over the world are growing and reaching out for more. Living prophets have urged, "Maintain an enthusiasm for learning throughout your life. Find joy in continuing to learn about yourself, other people, and the world around you. Study the words of the Lord, and continue learning about your Heavenly Father's plan" (*For the Strength of Youth,* 9).

Knowledge will help you in every aspect of your life. When you learn about many things, you are better able to make good decisions, help people in need, provide for your family now and in the future, and trust in the Lord. As we learn of Him, we are better able to hear the promptings of the Holy Spirit and to be guided to true joy. Even as we hunger for food, may our appetites for knowledge continually increase as well. May we never say "we've had enough," but let us be as a green, living tree—ever growing toward our Maker.

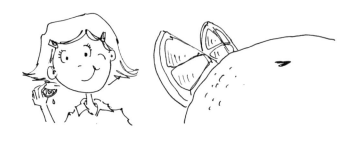

Choice and Accountability

Choice and Accountability is the sweetness of
An orange—
Reminding me that my wise choices
Bring forth good fruit.

We believe that we alone are accountable for our own sins (see A of F 2). Likewise, we will be rewarded for our wise choices. The consequences of these choices can be likened unto fruit. Have you ever bitten into an orange that was not yet ripe? The taste is bitter and sour. When you bite into fruit that is ripe, however, the taste is sweet and refreshing; its color is bright, and its taste delicious—much like an orange. Good fruit is the product of a wholesome tree. Likewise, as we continually make wholesome choices, the "fruit," or consequences, produced by these choices will be delicious. Like the fruit, the color orange represents Choice and Accountability, reminding us of the delicious reward of correct choices.

Our Agency, Our Blessing

Our agency, or the ability to choose for ourselves, is a blessing from the Lord. We may choose for ourselves to do right or wrong. This is part of the plan that Jesus Christ presented in the premortal realm, and we chose to live it. We learn from both our good and bad choices, but we must, however, accept accountability for all of them. Because God allows us to make our own decisions, we alone are responsible for the results of those decisions—whether those results be positive or negative.

When we choose to serve the Lord and do what is right, we are blessed. When we choose to disobey the Lord and disregard His commandments, we cannot have true joy. In Doctrine and Covenants 82:10, we read, "I, the Lord, am bound when ye do what I say; but when ye do not what I say, ye have no promise." He promises blessings if we follow His counsel and choose the right; but if we choose not to, He cannot extend those same blessings.

Many of us have known people who do their best to keep the commandments and are blessed for it. We also know others who openly break the Lord's commandments and are miserable because of it. Sometimes, however, we encounter people who do not appear to be keeping the commandments and yet seem to have money or fame or the appearance of happiness despite their poor choices. Rest assured that these people will eventually partake of their own *bitter* fruit. They will not be rewarded for bad choices—they cannot be. On the same note, the righteous who appear to have many trials will also eventually partake of their own *sweet* fruit. They *will be* rewarded for their faithfulness. Remember, the Lord said He is *bound*.

Alma teaches, "Ye shall reap the rewards of your faith, and your diligence, and patience, and long-suffering, waiting for the tree to bring forth fruit unto you" (Alma 32:43). Our good choices, in time, will *always* bring forth rewarding fruit.

Choosing the Right . . . and Standing for It

Some choices in life are easier to make than others. Many choices can be so difficult that we need to call upon the powers of heaven for strength. But through prayer and fasting, we can make the right choice with the Lord's help, no matter how difficult it may appear.

Queen Esther had an extremely difficult decision to make, one for which she'd be personally accountable—not only for her own safety, but for the safety of an entire people. Her story begins before she became a queen. When Esther was a young Jewish girl living with her cousin in Persia, King Ahasuerus brought the most beautiful women from his kingdom to the palace so that he could choose a new queen.

Esther, young and beautiful, was among the many women brought before the king. Eventually she was chosen to be the next queen of Persia. Esther proved herself to be a wise choice—not only for her beauty, but also for her wisdom and loyalty.

Some time later, a scandal arose in the kingdom. Because of an evil plot conceived by a man named Haman, the king became convinced that the Jews were not keeping his laws and must be destroyed. The king ordered that all Jews were to be killed. When Esther read this decree, she knew she had to act.

Esther was faced with a crucial choice. Royal law forbade anyone to approach the king without invitation, and Esther had not been invited to have an audience with him. She risked serious consequences, even death, by approaching him. However the king had ordered this decree, unaware that Esther herself was a Jew and that his trusted servant Haman had lied to him.

Esther chose to go to the king and plead for the lives of her people. Perhaps she felt scared and alone and worried about the king's reaction. Pushing her fears aside, Esther went to the king's court and bravely awaited his invitation or her death. The king did invite her to speak, and after Esther pleaded with him for the lives of her people, her request was granted. Both Esther and Haman were held accountable for their own choices—Esther's life was saved, Haman was put to death.

Esther's actions were bold and courageous, and she was able to feast on the sweet fruits of her wise choice—namely, saving her entire race. Because she stood up for herself and her people, Esther's choice will be eternally rewarded. Like Esther, when we stand up for ourselves and our values, we, too, make a courageous choice that will yield eternal rewards.

"Unpopularity" Is Only Temporary

Sometimes choosing the right—like dressing modestly, avoiding inappropriate media and activities, and dating at the appropriate age—is unpopular with the world.

It is hard at times to remember that this "unpopularity" is only temporary—but those that do "the works of righteousness shall receive [their] reward, even peace in this world, and eternal life in the world to come" (D&C 59:23). Living in this world with a clear conscience and a peaceful spirit is a valuable reward in itself.

For the Strength of Youth states, "While you are free to choose for yourself, you are not free to choose the consequences of your actions. When you make a choice, you will receive the consequences of that choice. The consequences may not be immediate, but they will always follow, for good or bad. Wrong choices delay your progression and lead to heartache and misery. Right choices lead to happiness and eternal life. That is why it is so important for you to choose what is right throughout your life" (4) Consequences from our poor choices will remain, and we all make mistakes. Thankfully, the heavy burden of sin can be lifted through the gift of repentance. The Lord has promised to take our burdens upon Himself through His atonement so that we may correct ourselves and again move forward choosing the right.

How to Choose?

Most of the time our choices are clear: there is a good option and a bad one. It is then simply up to us to choose the good. Sometimes, however, the options may both seem good, or perhaps they both seem bad and the decision is difficult to make. This is when we need to turn to the Lord for help. We must pray and fast, even as Esther did, for help not only in making wise choices, but also for help in dealing with the consequences of what we choose. For sometimes it takes great courage to do what is right. But we can take comfort, for as the well-known hymn teaches, "Do what is right; let the consequence follow . . . God will protect you; then do what is right" (*Hymns,* no. 237).

The Lord has given us laws and commandments to help us make correct choices which will bring us joy now and eventually lead us back to Him. It has been said that when we disobey God's law we are not really breaking the law but, rather, breaking ourselves against the law. God's laws exist to build us up and strengthen us. The choice to disobey God's laws only breaks us down and weakens us.

As we make wise choices, we grow in strength and spirit. We are then able to feast on "the peaceable fruit of righteousness" (Heb. 12:11). The color orange can remind us of the sweet and refreshing rewards we reap for choosing God's laws and obeying His will.

Good Works

Good Works is the yellow of
The sun
Spreading warmth to all in its reach.

We believe "in doing good to all men" (see A of F 13). Jesus Christ is not only our example but our partner in good works. Much like the Son of God, the earth's sun continuously shines upon us. Its yellow rays warm and nourish the earth, making life brighter. The best way for us to follow the Son and be like Him is to do our best to spread His light. Yellow, like the rays of the sun, is the color of Good Works.

We learn at an early age to sing the familiar words, "Jesus wants me for a sunbeam, To shine for him each day" (*Primary Children's Songbook,* 60). Being a sunbeam for Him means spreading His light over the whole earth through our good works and service to others. The First Presidency of the Church introduces the Personal Progress program with these words: "Use your influence to lift and bless your family, other young women, and the young men with whom you associate. Honor womanhood, support the priesthood, and treasure faithful motherhood and fatherhood" *(Young Women Personal Progress,* 1). No matter how old or young we are, we have a responsibility to scatter sunshine by loving, giving, and doing good to all. Our influence as young women of God can be the light that brightens even the darkest day.

Many people pray for help from heaven each day, and through the Savior's valiant "sunbeams," those prayers may be answered. It is a wonderful blessing to be the answer to someone's prayer, the reason for someone's smile, or the light in someone's life. How great it is to add a little light to the world each day through our example and good works. It follows, of course, that as we scatter sunshine, we in turn illuminate our own path and bid the darkness to flee.

Women of Good Works

To be sure, there are countless women who have accomplished great things themselves and to whom we can look to as examples of good works, but we must also honor the many selfless women who give of their time, talents, and everything they can to support the Lord's anointed. These are the mothers, wives, and daughters of the prophets. The love, support, and nurturing these women provide helps to make these men who they are—instruments of God in moving the work of the Lord forward. Of the numerous women who may be found on this list, two who stand out in early Church history are Lucy Mack Smith, the mother of Joseph Smith, and the Prophet's good wife, Emma Smith.

Lucy Mack Smith

Long before Lucy Mack Smith gave birth to young Joseph, she lived a life of good works. Yet as the mother of this choice spirit, she added much light to his life as he grew and became the first prophet of the latter days. From the tender age of fourteen, when Joseph had his incredible first vision, Lucy Mack supported, believed in, and defended her prophet son with admirable strength and steadfastness. She never doubted that he had seen Heavenly Father and Jesus Christ.

Lucy Mack was very interested in religion herself and had investigated many churches. She may have been the example Joseph followed when he went into the woods to pray. Her son William said that Lucy made "use of every means which her parental love could suggest to get us engaged in seeking for our souls' salvation" (Richard Lyman Bushman, *Joseph Smith: Rough Stone Rolling*, 26). She raised each of her children to learn of God and His ways and to do good to their fellow men. She cooked and cleaned and loved and helped Joseph, as well as each of his siblings. But most importantly, she stood by Joseph—even during unimaginably difficult times.

Emma Smith

As Emma joined the Smith family, she also spread sunshine in their lives. Lucy and Emma loved each other, and they both loved Joseph. Emma had the daunting task of lightening the load of the Prophet and husband she loved. Emma moved many times, endured many challenges, and lost many loved ones as she supported and stood beside her husband. At one lonely point in his tumultuous life when Joseph was in hiding, Emma came to visit him. He wrote of the occasion:

> With what unspeakable delight, and what transports of joy swelled in my bosom, when I took by the hand, on that night, my beloved Emma—she that was my wife, even the wife of my youth, and the choice of my heart. Many were the reverberations of my mind when I contemplated for a moment the many scenes we had been called to pass through, the fatigue and toils, the sorrows and sufferings, and the joys and consolations, from time to time, which had strewed our paths and crowned our board. Oh what a commingling of thought filled my mind for the moment, again she is here, even in the seventh trouble—undaunted, firm, and unwavering—unchangeable, affectionate, Emma! (*History of the Church*, 5:107)

Not only did she shine her light on so many of the Prophet's darkest days, but she also brightened the lives of many others. As the first president of the Relief Society organization, Emma Smith began a legacy that has grown immeasurably, blessing people all over the world for generations. Both Emma and Lucy, along with many others, shine for us today as examples of the good each of us can do.

Our Own "Special Kind of Good"

Women in general have a unique ability to do our own special kind of good. We can see the need for comfort and service. We can reach out in a way that is warm, tender, and inviting. Elder M. Russell Ballard of the Quorum of the Twelve Apostles has said the following concerning our unique influence:

My dear sisters, you have a profound, innate spiritual ability to hear the voice of the Good Shepherd. . . . Never doubt that your influence is absolutely vital to preserving the family and to assisting with the growth and spiritual vitality of the Church. This Church will not reach its foreordained destiny without you. We men simply cannot nurture as you nurture. Most of us don't have the sensitivity, spiritual and otherwise, that by your eternal nature you inherently have. Your influence on families and with children, youth and men is singular. You are natural-born nurturers. Because of these unusual gifts and talents, you are vital to taking the gospel to all the world, to demonstrating that there is joy in living the way prophets have counseled us to live. ("Women of Righteousness," *Ensign*, April 2002, 66–73)

We should never be afraid to help when we see a need. There is a lot of bad in our world, but there is also much good. We can add to that good every day, thus vanquishing a little of the bad at the same time. We can look around and find ways to change the world, one small act of kindness at a time.

It has been said that when you help someone else, you help yourself, and it is so true. How can you not smile a little when you have made a crying child laugh? Or how can you not feel good inside when you have shared the good news of the gospel with someone you love? Good works are just that: good. They make you feel good, they make others feel good. As we serve others we help the Savior spread His light to all the earth . . . including to ourselves.

Like Emma and Lucy Mack Smith, we can find joy in good works. Although they experienced heartrending trials, we also know that for these women, life was not void of happiness. They laughed and loved and sang and danced. They must have also experienced great joy through their good works—and they now have moved on to an even greater joy in the eternities. And we can carry on their legacy and join them as women of good works.

In 3 Nephi 12:16 the Savior asks us to follow this commandment: "Therefore let your light so shine before this people, that they may see your good works and glorify your Father who is in heaven." Just as we all count on the sun to rise every day and warm us with its rays, may the Lord also count on us to rise every day determined to do our very best to warm hearts and brighten the world with His love. May the cheery yellow light of a sunshiny day inspire us to "make [a] pathway bright, fill[ing] soul[s] with heaven's light" (*Hymns,* no. 228).

Integrity

*Integrity is the purple of
Royalty
From where I have come,
And to which I will someday return.*

"If there is anything virtuous, lovely, or of good report or praiseworthy, we seek after these things" (A of F 13). The final value young women seek to implement in their lives is Integrity, represented by the color purple. Value number seven is the product of living the other six. As we strive to live faith, divine nature, individual worth, knowledge, choice and accountability, and good works, we gain integrity. It is our personal integrity that keeps us from jeopardizing our other values. President Gordon B. Hinckley states, "In all this world there is no substitute for personal integrity. It includes honor. It includes performance. It includes keeping one's word. It includes doing what is right regardless of the circumstances" (*Teachings of Gordon B. Hinckley,* 270).

Because we are daughters of royal birth, preparing to one day return to our royal heritage, we act accordingly. Like the purple robes often worn by royalty, a young woman of integrity is clothed in a royal "robe of righteousness" (2 Ne. 9:14). We are born as royalty and we must commit as Job to never forsake our divine heritage. "Till I die I will not remove mine integrity from me" (Job 27:5).

Heaven's royalty lives uprightly and does not waiver in keeping the commandments. A daughter of God with integrity is honest and true in times of darkness and in times of light. As His royal daughter, she speaks, dresses, and acts accordingly. She behaves the same whether in a crowd or in a private moment alone because she knows exactly who she is. Her integrity blesses those around her, glorifies her Father in Heaven, and strengthens herself.

The Savior's mother, Mary, was such a woman. She led an exceptional life. We know that as a young woman she looked forward to the day when the Messiah would come—long before it was revealed that *she* would be His mother. To have been entrusted with this role, Mary must have lived her life honestly and uprightly at all times. Truly, she must have spoken, dressed, and acted according to her faith—a woman of the most profound integrity. The angel Gabriel visited Mary and said to her, "Hail, thou art highly favoured, the Lord is with thee: blessed art thou among women" (Luke 1:28). She, out of every other woman who had or would ever live, was chosen to bear the Savior of the world.

We know through the scriptural account that young Mary was espoused to Joseph the carpenter; they had not yet wed. To be an unmarried woman with child in their culture was a cause for great shame. But Mary knew she would be fulfilling the will of God, and so she was willing to bear that burden and any other that would come along in order to fulfill God's plan for her. After the angel had delivered his message, Mary simply replied, "Behold the handmaid of the Lord; be it unto me according to thy word" (Luke 1:38).

Mary wanted nothing more than to do the will of the Lord, whatever it may have been. The scriptures tell us but a few things that she experienced as the mother of Jesus. Although it was surely a joyous experience, it must have been incredibly difficult. Imagine the burden and responsibility of raising the Savior of the world, even your own Savior. But she was true to her Father in Heaven, she was true to her Savior and son, and she was true to herself.

Mary is and always will be honored for her life of integrity. She was a daughter of the King, chosen to beget His royal Son. Righteous and steadfast in her mission, she never wavered in her purpose. Like Mary, each young woman is a chosen daughter of God who must live royally to fulfill her own unique mission. This is how we confirm our place in His royal courts on high, dressed as Mary and all those who have lived uprightly and honorably, we too will be "clothed with [royal] robes of righteousness" (D&C 29:12).

Conclusion

The Young Women values with their corresponding colors can help us to seek after those things that are "virtuous, lovely, or of good report," as the Savior would have us do. Each value plays an important role, not only in our personal progress, but in our mission to help others come unto Christ. The colors which represent each value can be seen throughout God's creations—they're daily reminders of these powerful truths. As we live the Young Women values, we too become daily reminders, for those we come in contact with, of the Savior's mission—His creation, His life, and His Atonement. It is now our blessing to live these values for Him.

FAITH is the white of
Sacred clothing
So pure and clean—
Blessing, baptism, and temple.

DIVINE NATURE is the blue of the
The clearest sky
Reminding me of my heavenly home.

INDIVIDUAL WORTH is the red of
A single rose—
Bold, unique, and beautiful.

KNOWLEDGE is the green of
A living tree
Whose growth has made it strong.

CHOICE AND ACCOUNTABILITY is the sweetness of
An orange—
Reminding me that my wise choices
Bring forth good fruit.

GOOD WORKS is the yellow of
The sun
Spreading warmth to all in its reach.

INTEGRITY is the purple of
Royalty
From where I have come,
And to which I will someday return.